Everyone Lives Here

Poems
Art
Sharon Webster

Fomite Press
Burlington, VT

Poems and art copyright 2014 © by Sharon Webster
Cover art & photo by Sharon Webster

All rights reserved. No part of this book may be reproduced in any form or by any means without the prior written consent of the publisher, except in the case of brief quotations used in reviews and certain other noncommercial uses permitted by copyright law.

ISBN-13: 978-1-937677-70-1
Library of Congress Control Number: 2014942472

Fomite
58 Peru Street
Burlington, VT 05401
www.fomitepress.com

For my partner, Dave

&
in joyful memory
of my parents

Acknowledgments

Many thanks to the editors who published these poems:

"Resistance" in *So Little Time - Words and Images for a World in Climate Crisis,* Green Writers Press.

"What Dirt Smells Like" and "L'Eau" in *The Salon, Honeybee Press.*

"Weeping In the Kmart Premenstrual" in *Green Mountains Review.*

"It's Rising" in *Take Heart* and *Seven Days.*

"The Cleaning Lady" in *The Burlington Review.*

~

Much gratitude to Sue Burton for her ongoing support, vision, and expert editorial advice. Also for her laughter, water on a hot day.

Deep thanks to Dave Cavanagh and Greg Delanty for their many insights and suggestions regarding my work and their consistent urging me to go public.

Thanks to Patti Ferreria for her ebullient self and for pushing me on.

Heartfelt thanks to Donna Bister and Marc Estrin of Fomite Press for their ingenious work in publishing that embraces, art, community and a mysterious, third other. They truly have created a contagion.

Thank you, Mrs. Mary Broberg, for saving my bacon in high school art class.

Finally, I salute my teacher, the inimitable Bob Paterson of Hawk Junction, Ontario (1936-2013), whose playful passion and spirit of invention touched countless lives and rises still.

A loaded baseball diamond lives inside everyone
while a tiny reflection of grass in the window tells a long story
to keep my heart
afloat.

Contents

Spring

Start	1
It's Rising	3
Wings!	4
Image - "Want In"	5
What Dirt Smells Like:	6
Turn This Corner	8
Is Ballet	9
Yes	10
Temple Grandin	11
Meditation On Locust Street	13
Lima Beans	15
Image - "Urge - The Wheel"	16
Gladiolus Bulbs / Peaches	17
Springtime After His Heart Surgery	18
On The Dingle Peninsula, Ireland	20
Whatever Else I Am Doing These Days	21

Summer

L'Eau	25
On The Sidewalk, Practicing	*26*
I Want A Flagrant Dream	27
Weeping In The Kmart, Premenstrual	28
Enjoy	30
It's A James Schuyler Fourth	31
Image - "Tom Box"	32
Tomorrow It Will Probably Be Hard To Get Up But Tell Me Anyway	34
The Day That Russel Died	36
The Cleaning Lady	37
After The Hysterectomy	40
Image - "Loom"	44
Soulwork	45
Midpoint	46

Fall

Bruised Feet	51
Image - "Root"	52
Rosh Hashana	53
Art Teacher Decodes The Art Supplies	54
O Planet	56
The Way They're Built	57
In The Dream	59
Image - "Mind and Matter"	60
After The Wind	61
The Kingdom Of God Is Within, So What	62
Finish /Unfinish	63
Two Novembers	64
Almost Thanksgiving, Unsteady	65
I Have The Sunset, Pink	68
With Everyone	69

Winter

At The Studio	75
Ah, To Think Of Rilke In The Locker Room	76
Reach Ecstasy	77
Why I Love Your Face	78
Yellowed Sun	79
Drawing Class Model	80
The Visit / Old Friend, Lost	82
Vacant Sky	83
Breath / Work / Birds	85
Image - "Labille Guiard"	86
The Music Of Their Names	87
No More Pragmatic Notes	88
Image - "Paintbrush Wheel"	89
Resistance	90
The Moon Is A Still	91
Napkin Poems	92

Spring

Start. 	Start with opening. 	Start.

Start with the window. 	Start.

	Start with the
	simple. Start

with the strength.

	Start with opening. 	Start

	with the window.

Start with opening

	the window.

IT'S RISING

She wakes up and starts to
look at things. Everything is a strange
capsule of beauty, rich and compact. Peacock
feathers in a vase have deep blue rings and shimmer
with many aqua - green eyes that fall gently out
and down, but also up. Each strand glows in
a slow bath of half-night, half-light. Outside
the window, the edges of the lilac leaves cut
hearts in the white August fog. Fragile
elbows of light lie on the man and
the woman waiting inside.

It's about being unimpressed
and impressed at the same time. It's about
letting the length of something go on for
a long while. It's about being *in* the vase
with the peacock feathers while
someone holds your ankles and
you fall gently out and
down, but also up.

WINGS!

Every door she opened in those days
held wings. It didn't

       matter where. It was always the entrance.
       She pushed the door and a burst of gray

    feathers flew in all directions. Starlings
    from the doorbell, sparrows from the gutter,

      pigeons from the eaves. It happened
      everywhere, the homes of friends, in

   stores, work, the library. In those days
   the doors were feathers. Every door

she opened held wings. Not
hers, just wings.

Anonymous. Something flew
when she pushed the door.

Want In — mixed media

WHAT DIRT SMELLS LIKE:

deep thunder, layers
of mink

stole, chocolate
cake, crumbled

trees, human
blood,

one-third
of your life, the opposite

of sky, sleep's
thirsty floor,

silver
and worms

working it under,
under and in-

side and out, a bed.

WHEN THE GRASS
comes up

it is abrupt
wine, it

is sudden teeth,
sky from

exact
green inner,

you could
eat it

this wild,
huge earth

has white teeth
pulling.

TURN THIS CORNER

like everyone lives here.
The collected dark

is where you start.
Your spine

knows itself
in the slow

drop of temperature
on the stairs

the changing grays
are how you breathe

and how you hold
the shifting

air. The shared

descent in
everyone's grip

is a handhold
held by

everyone's climb.
Step after step

is everyone's name.

IS BALLET

People finding their garden
hoses under shrubbery at the end
of the day, the nozzle cool, the "shush" sound of water
falling
is ballet. People tending
anything, working past dark, the sound of water
falling on warm dirt.
Throwing
yourself   into   the   great   silence
while looking at everything
ballet   ballet   ballet.
Movement and moist
remembering the absolute, unflinching way
it continues. Many
young people in one room,
ballet
working past dark, the river
the jazz made
through the air.
Turning
on the stairs with a bowl full
of popcorn   is
is
is

YES

I have a special outlook on life.
It comes from the dirt.

It takes its name from the
way the rain sounds when it won't

stop, won't stop, won't stop. It
is the color of an oyster, a slug,

a dirt fist. It makes its home
in my most alone. It is the

secret pact that really isn't
secret, but I pretend it is

for the sake of the outlook.
It is the shape of a bird, an old

woman and the creases beside
both of your eyes. It

redesigns everything, plans
my escape. When you see me

again I will be black, shiny muscle,
maniac crow. I will be efficient

and snap like a ruler. You will
take me seriously.

TEMPLE GRANDIN

Her name came to me as we talked,
my old friend who was,
like Temple, "on the spectrum." That's
the phrase they
use now to say
autism means many
things, not one.
Here in the grocery store with my
friend and her loyal sister
who nudges, "We say hello
to people we know, Cindy…" it came back. Temple's
name had eluded
me for weeks. I could see but not say the heroic
woman in her cowboy collar who
feels what the animals feel. *Temple Grandin*,
a large Jewish church
is a good way to remember Temple who
senses what is
invisible to others, patterns
as animals feel them, see them by-
passing all that literal
surface to *see* where
others merely look. Now

I remember the round

red circles that my friend

painted, fueled

from the elbow — as much a

dance of the arm

as a spreading of color.

Always on the hot

spectrum: orange pink red maroon

were her choices. Hot suns

where others saw paint

she saw suns

on fire like the larger pattern

we make moving

and going.

Her eyes large, a temple.

Temple Grandin (b.1947) is an autism activist and American professor of animal science. She herself is a person with autism. Her work on autism and the humane treatment of farm animals is ground-breaking and has won numerous awards and international recognition.

MEDITATION ON LOCUST STREET

Because it is May, stop the car
and take off your socks. Watch

the green rain
dribble green patterns, slow

down the windshield, tree
trunks become liquid

smears. Across the street,
a hundred blossoms

leap in the branches, opening
the sky. Now moistened, reach

for the ignition, then
watch something else: a wet

playground, a pizza delivery
man finding his doorbell. Admire

how uncut
someone's lawn is. Tiny

white violets sprout like
earlobes in the silky

new grass, unplanted
petunias wait

on a stoop. It's all
thawed out, it doesn't

stop and you want to
wash yourself in this mounting

warmth, take off what's
hard and leave yourself

here in the loosened
green on Locust Street.

I lie here and let the lima beans grow
down here with the allergens I think
it is a good disguise the sun
pushes blood through my body, lets
me think like a vegetable. Look: The
window is more shapely this year than
last and it's no accident the cat
forgets he's separate from the grasses
watch   the shadows forgive him.

                    You
              watch everything
       revolve around the white snapdragons
     in a glass of water, long stalks and careful
              of small, air-filled birds,
                 connective
          notes from a bell, bubbles, they
              tell you keep going, they
               tell you be careful
               they tell you   they
                  tell you.

Urge - The Wheel — mixed media

```
                    The
        GLADIOLUS
                    BULBS leak

    eager color from their papery hearts, loose
                        red
                          in my hands. I
          put them in the earth     and hope
                       for blood.




        CLING PEACHES
                &
        SAUERKRAUT
    A package of unopened Cosmos:
              a whole day
               to do it in.
```

SPRINGTIME AFTER HIS HEART SURGERY

All the different
bird sounds.

I want there to be
birdsong

while we make love.
I want there to be

birdsong while

magic is alive
and completely human,

full of wonder
and one sound.

The glare off the parked car
before dawn.

Borrowed thought.
Longing

for your roomy
intelligence, generous

reactions. Sighs.

Jim says, "To tell you the truth

I think he has a big thing
for Kim." In the student evaluations,

it should read *exceeds
expectations.*

Sweating and tossing,
coolness

later on. The lonely
parked car. The glare.

Streetlight.

Waiting
in the house

for him. My own
rhythms.

The bus to Montreal.

His gentle
boyhood, soft

on a street with a
French name. His pain.

So many openings.
A rest. His heart.

His heart.

Green continues
through the slanted

window frame, an
opening.   A

wedge.

ON THE DINGLE PENINSULA, IRELAND

    It was there with the old
stones, you opened me a

    new way, the green
dead mothers coming in. You were the

    mortar, a motor, inventor,
a boat. I spread and became

    light of day, am a day, the passing
of sun between what looked like

    brand new leaves.

WHATEVER ELSE I AM DOING THESE DAYS

I am really thinking about my mother.
A wedge of shadow squeezes under the bedroom door, widens
and shrinks like a tent of darkness
attached to light, like her.
How good
to wake up and love the abandoned night,
to move
through the shadows,
not afraid because of her. How rich
this
under my fingernails,
how fertile this
opening
she gave me and how to make everything
fit it.

Summer

L'EAU

It was the way I could hear her
even when I couldn't hear her.

It was her voice in the water, so
cold that it stung. It was the snow-

ball bush in the front yard, drunk
on its own runny sweetness. It

was her arm over her head like
she was reaching for something.

It was moving like that. It was
the center of the earth in each

of her foot soles. It was finally
warm enough. It was her breath

growing mothlike and furred in the
mirror. It was the weight of her

hair. It was her hair, period. It
was the way that I knew her full

of promise and futile. It was
something about salt.

It was moving.

ON THE SIDEWALK, PRACTICING, *for Dave*

A slash of mud across my calf, flattened

light in the window: What color

from the bottom
of a puddle? Blue

letters up a pole
spell

    B   U   S

                but I'm not
                going anywhere.

That's you
catching the next constellation.

And thanks
for privacy
                in the open
                and orbits
                in my foot soles.
    At home

                without knowing,
                you invent
eternity again, and

        the soft room
        in your eye

                where I loosen
                where I root.

I WANT A FLAGRANT DREAM

    tonight, magenta, ripe

    orange streaks
    to sop up my mind, purple

stains in all the cracks. I want to scratch
                          the black sky

and get Venus
out of it. I want
the black sky   in reverse

under my fingernails. I
want it
        flaming and
            fevered for miles. I

want the better
flushed light

            of darkness.
I want it livid tonight.
                I want to rip it
    to shreds and
        leave it

            outlandish.

WEEPING IN THE KMART, PREMENSTRUAL

parking lot. Seat-belted next to me,
my companion

has early Alzheimer's and Down Syndrome.
The radio sings, not Armatrading, but in a similar

tonal zone, simmering in the deep parts,
turning like a roiling boat, a slave ship.

"Who will save your soul...?"
sings the woman

from the dashboard, and
a million days are re-created. The ache

of complexity: A wet
berry of pain, a hanged human voice. *Is this*

a joke job, or a real job? Is this a joke
life or a real life? Jackie

has forgotten why we've come. So much
forgetting. Time and place are darkened

now, a wall of no-context, the backside
of a mirror. You need great

inventiveness when you
forget everything. You need great

inventiveness and you accept
the most marvelous of things

as each moment presents its blankness.
Jackie does this, but it's tiring

for her, too. It's tiring for her,
so she remembers me

and lets me pull her along. She
remembers me and hovers on my arm

like one of those air-filled balls
at the end of a fishing line. I tug

her to the surface while the
Alzheimer hook-and-sinker

pulls her down. Every moment
brings more gravity, farther down, but

I work hard to imagine air.
I imagine air and pull her up. I pull her up,

and she bobs there perilously,
part of both worlds. Now,

the woman on the radio
is singing about hitting the street,

the bills to pay, forever struggle, and the
universal butt worked off.

"Who will save your soul?"

I turn off the ignition, the voice
dissolves and we go in.

ENJOY

    her legs
    crossed
    like that: sort of
    brown flesh
    on more sort of
    brown flesh, two
    crooks, the
    necks
    of dolphins bent
    like these
    businessmen
    who fill the tiny plane
    with aftershave
    and sweet morning air.
    Rivers bloom through the window into raised
    blue
    sky while you ascend quietly strange
    flowers
    nest in your lungs.

IT'S A JAMES SCHUYLER FOURTH

          of July. Breathe.
The wide

          side of a truck
          is full of sensuality
          and loose
          connotation. It reads

          "BLUE SKY FURNISHINGS,
                    RECAPTURE."
And it makes   sense

that if I
still dream about
          Tommy Moon and his
          mean motorcycle he may still

dream of me. Way down
          in Kentucky, he
          wakes up

          in his mobile home and says out loud
          my name.
          The old guy

          is practically
          a hermit now, but comes to me
in dreams

as that painfully shy,
          foul-mouthed youth
          I wistfully gave my virginity to
          many years ago. So

          much we shared: our
          consummate

fragility, he would
> pull the car over and puke
> out the door
> every time we had a fight.

> And I, perpetually
bruised
> by the hoopla
> of high school and
> upstanding

> family expectations.

But along with that, we shared

> the peculiar
> iron of outcasts.

> And along with that,
a luxuriant humor. We laughed,

> loafed, heartily invited
> our souls   And this

> morning when my husband asks
> what
> time is it? Tommy

> speaks through me: "Half past a
> monkey's ass." Ah, Tommy, I hold you

> still.

---

*James Schuyler (pronounced *Sky-ler)* (1923-1991) was an American poet whose work often contained sensual details from ordinary life described in a vivid, visual way.

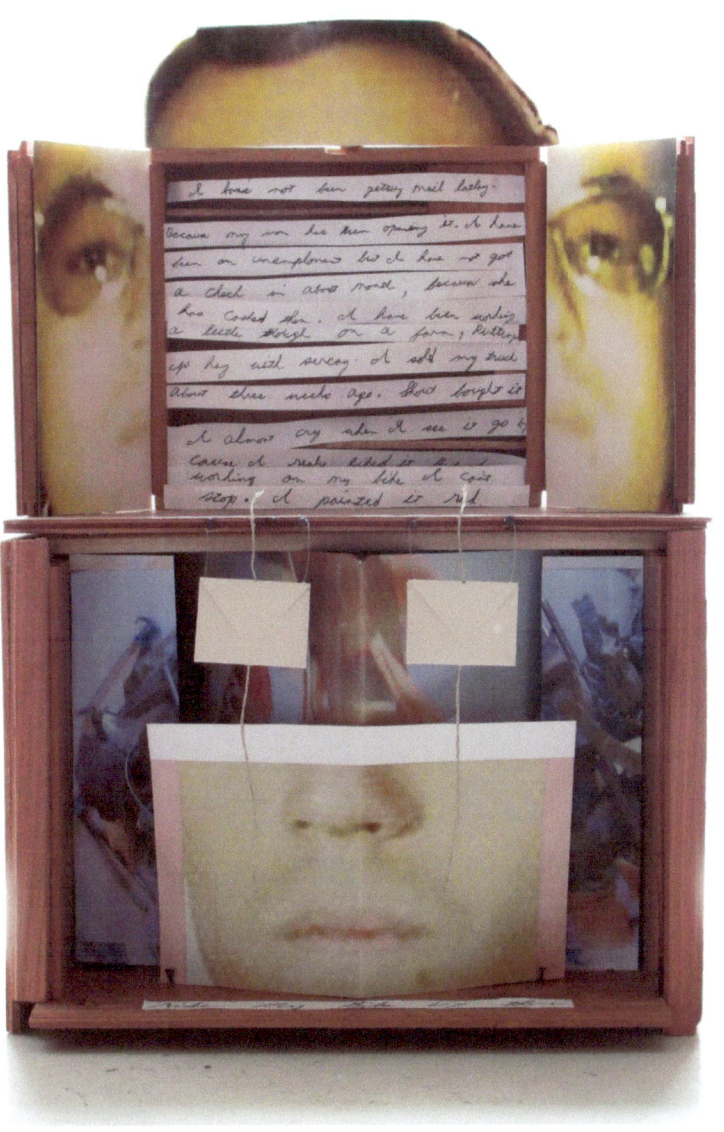

Tom Box — mixed media

TOMORROW IT WILL PROBABLY BE HARD TO GET UP BUT TELL ME ANYWAY

There's not much to be surprised about now. The rain
that is falling was predicted well
in advance. "A storm tonight," was
how the radio put it. Serves us right.
No surprises.
The window shade shifts
and slouches over the black
yawn of the open window. Moves
like someone is out there breathing.
Real even, regular breaths. So what?
asks the night.
My great-grandmother chewed tobacco and shot long
streams of muscular, brown juice
into a pedaled
wastebasket that squawked
every time her foot
cocked it open. She had
fingers long as candlesticks and knuckles like loose
marbles. She could shoot
a rifle, once shot
a man for robbing the family
tavern – for taking
money made from countless
chickens fried in iron skillets big as tabletops.
Shot him, but he deserved it, making
her only son's wife lay, nine
months pregnant, all over the cold restaurant floor.

That was the Depression. Things
like that happened; they were used to it.
My middle name is for her, Elizabeth. But
they called her Bessie. She
lost her teeth around thirty, her
husband before that. Never replaced
either. Wore
her hair in cold black waves
till she died at ninety-three.
There's a photograph I think of: She's belting back something
from a long-necked bottle, her body a
long sling-shot, tough
and graceful, an easy curve cocky as any man. So what?
asks the night. I was born like this.
But when I think of Bessie
I am tall. Like her,
my finger
reaches the trigger.

THE DAY THAT RUSSEL DIED

I had menstrual cramps in the dark

house while the sky

> cracked and too much water
> came down loud.
> My pain was a partner
> of pure light
> that I trusted

implicitly and moved

> with. My pain was evidence
> and utterance of life. It was
> summer and sudden.
> It was August
> and the room
> was a high-ceilinged cavity
> made of danger, a

darkness I could taste. The taste

> of rain was tin that day. The rain
> was old.

THE CLEANING LADY

1.

The cleaning lady
tries hard to be invisible.
She slinks past your wedding
pictures, tries not to look: Your
stilted smiles, lace,
all that gullible promise
erect in your invincible
teeth. You glare at her,
safe in your four-cornered
world. You say, "Look.
We have made it. We are
happy. We are not like you."
She slams your faces
into the piano.

2.

Don't try to kid yourself
that she doesn't resent you.
She resents everything about you:
Your orderly houseplants,
pictures of your parents, pathetic
cereal bowls, still wet
with brand names you eat,
over-stuffed sofas, your *Time*
magazines lined
up like dominos.

She hates your dog.

3.

She will not forgive you.
You have pushed her
too long into the
vacuum, bribed her
with politeness, "Please
pay special attention
to the furniture. Use attachments."

4.

She has had it. That's
the phrase that goes over
and over in her head, insidious
time bomb, a saw.
But her head's not
wood, it hurts. Her
resentment sits
on her lips; she can't
spit it out. Day after
day she imagines her eyes
becoming rags, rung out
too many times
against the sun. She
thinks about the creases.

5.

The cleaning lady tries hard,
though. There must be something
in even this, some beauty
beneath the dirt.
Is a clean bathtub
like a sonnet or a sunset? The last
pubic hair
slithering down the drain.

AFTER THE HYSTERECTOMY

Now I'm latching
onto it. Everything
that happens is a victory.
That it is today
and not yesterday is one.

~

I'm getting used to it. Who
are you
when you dream?
Yourself, but younger?
Yourself, but older?
Yourself, but elsewhere?
When you dream you are the most yourself
you ever get. Maybe.

~

Dave is cutting the grass.
The sound is half-
custodial, half-
celestial. Its
useful clatter cheers and remembers me.

The shade licking
the bottom
of the maple tree is another
thing to hang onto. Even

this broken
condition is just as it should be.
Imperfection

is its own reward. Imperfection
is a favorable
position
to observe the extraordinary. Maybe.

~

Next day is harder. Dave
lifts me onto the bed, then
there's the ache,

the place
where the womb came out.

Dave is rebuilding
the front porch. He

takes out the old, ant-eaten wood
and puts in fresh, rot-resistant

wood, treated and measured
ahead of time. The nails

he pulls from the old wood
are curled and rusted, like

fossilized teeth. The new wood is tinted green,
permanently fresh. Dave pounds

the boards in at just the right angle. He hopes
they will stay awhile.

~

July is growing flags of grass
and my heart is elastic
with joy when
the sun through your
straw hat
breaks your face
into tiny squares of light and great
escape.

~

I know it's today and I know it's July 22, but who's counting?
One
small lily has yet to bloom beyond the window.
Things are feeling better, now
is not over. It is
many things. Many
is better than some things. Seventeen
is how many years Dave
and I have been married and I'm looking forward to more
beer and caviar, a little candlelight
and it looks good in the newspaper. They had a parade
on Church Street because the clarinet man died. People
were fond of him because he followed his own shtick
and a statue of him
in his favorite scarf
might not be a bad
idea. When the
saints come in is a number we all know
together. My favorite holy
place is Canada with crisp trees
that push the sky up and up with so much pure
space and rock islands, karma you
can move in. People, too. I hope the whole
world is well with wellfulness but what
can you do? What nationality
is "Wegner?" I wondered
on the operating table, as in: *Dr. Wegner is my gynecologist*,
but all she said was "I thought the old Champ was nice."
German? Dutch, maybe? The most amazing
thing was that during surgery I could see
my own thighs in the reflections
on the overhead O. R. lamps. Four
orderly Rorschach's,
one for each lamp. I am

promising to do good things
forever if I ever get better, i.e. deserve
my betterness. Practice good works and charity
ad nauseam. Many fine
people are not well. It is true and not
comfortable. I didn't
look for long.

~

September is schitzy; it's mixed
salt and sugar. Hard cider
on the ripened
fields. Wild
red abundance.
Cool fire and coming end. End
and open.
End. Breathe
light. Night
comes and
cry.

Loom — mixed media

SOULWORK

The sorrow

of this beautiful
summer evening:

the homeless people
are dancing too. Toothless

and unbathed, little pockmarks on the asphalt

dangerous music from the windows
no books cigarettes.

MIDPOINT

I am a season of constant change.
> I am storms.
> I am

a season of mistakes, missteps and missed
> hunches.

I am joyful in fits and starts.

> I am seasoned.
> I am unadorned.

I am the minute without my name on it. I

> am prepared. I am
> improvising

> the end of pragmatism.
> I am walking in spite of the pain.

I am in love and hate at the same time.

> I am watchful.
> I am assisted living.

I am putting the recycling out.

> I am a chorus.
> I am alone.

I am magnifying

>   the three red veins
>   in the maple leaf.

I am enlarging the rain. I am trying to see

>   this way,
>   then the path

of the hardwired trees. I am more like a
    weed than a flower.

I am black cohosh. I am bleeding.

>   I am finished.
>   I have not begun.

Fall

BRUISED FEET

This September
morn-
ing. Not
as much dread,
out of the deep
sheets of
night's connective
nest. Not
one season
leaves
the next, but
rather tugged
by the same
exquisite
thread, all
night the
little
trees snaking
through my
dreams, dancing
their long
lacy
decay while
slowly
awake
women watch
every morning
bleached a paler
yellow, edges
cracked
& buoyant,
stirred toward their
more elegant (airborne
death.

Root — mixed media

ROSH HASHANA

They walk toward sundown
and then they walk back –

the row of men in dark
round hats, broken

sunlight rolled into the brims, softly
into their hats. And

the men are walking slowly.
The men are rolling downhill

where sundown collects. The
men are falling

into the bowl
of all shadow. Summer built

this temple
and they walk toward it.

Summer's heaped
the flowers just

so something golden
could crack this

autumnal day, this
buttered, yellow scene,

unseen
before the sun melts.

And the men are dark.
And the men are very

solitary.

And the men are walking
together.

ART TEACHER DECODES THE ART SUPPLIES
(What She Brought for Them)

Chicken wire.
>Lowly, but strong,
bent on protection
in an infinity of shapes
an embankment,
a container for their thoughts.

Needles.
>Their bright.
Their useful bite.
Their methodical.
Their danger
and the opportunity
for repair
that they held out.

Glue.
>The recipe
for a strong one, the pleasure
of pouring
very slow. The surrendered
skin of fingertips
and the liquid
quality of attachment.

Linseed oil.
>Its golden color
and mysterious purpose. Its
rich odor and ability
to increase what it touches
and move.

A roll of drawings
> rescued
> and resuscitated
> from the tyranny
> of pragmatic thought.

Mirrors
> with sturdy frames
> for portraits
> of verbs and
> inner attributes.
> What the soul gave back.

The texture
> of papier mache,' its ripped
> its gold-seasoned
> time massaged
> and smoothed,
> water and wheat.
> The smell of earth,
> the smell of heat.

Name tags.
> The cheer of the blue-bordered *Hello,*
> *I'm...* stuck on the lint of her sweater.
> Its crooked start

> sensuous pigment or caked tubes.
> A book of symbols. Invisible ink.

Plastic mixing bowls the colors of every crayon
> in the box.

> The freedom to be imperfect.
> The freedom to get it right.

O PLANET,

you are not linear
or easy to explain. A thousand shades of blue
and the slow sun
blurring everything,
turning over
turning
in. Oh planet, one loose shadow
is enough
to make me forget
the dark awhile and sing.

THE WAY THEY'RE BUILT

Flesh-colored flowers
lean against burgundy
against yellow

like steps, the way they're built, a
sequence, a staggered
structure that says: Enter. Come in.
Move on.
The path is friendly
but moving. The path is made

out of flesh-colored corners
and piles
of flowers that work on each other like
steps, like staggered
notes, the way they're built.

They bend
when the wind
like a rag
wraps around the house
and the night is tossed,
and the bushes wrestle
with their backs that way. The bushes

say: It is probably
not time for us, but I

wish it was
wish it was
wish it was.

The steps, the way they're built:
logical and leading
to a conclusion, leaning
on each other, resisting

but holding still.

The way the wind
is built

and it probably isn't
time for us, but I
wish it was
wish it was
wish it was.

IN THE DREAM

I.
In the dream it was a totem pole.
In the dream there was more than one.
In the dream we were working together.

II.
In the dream it was stubborn.
In the dream it resisted
completion; it wanted to be a clothes rack
or a croquet mallet.
In the dream it would not be built.

III.
In the dream it was a penis.
It was strapped to my waist
or surgically attached.
In the dream it was a soft nozzle,
a nose. In the dream
it could smell me.

IV.
In the dream it was a dance.
In the dream it was a dance I invented
and it moved both ways.
In the dream I was leaning
into them.
In the dream I filled
and felt.
In the dream I was a pattern.
I repeated and grew.

V.
In the dream I was walking
toward the totem, the penis,
the dance. In the dream
I was carrying it off.

Mind and Matter — mixed media

AFTER THE WIND

>   your kiss is apple
>   cider   whiskey apricot
>   around my tongue somewhere
>   before   winter
>   i memorize
>   your   body   and
>   its pale
>   dawn   its   drowning
>   around   such   moist.

THE KINGDOM OF GOD IS WITHIN, SO WHAT

is all this other stuff? A squashed
crabapple under my foot, a huge
zucchini, the excellence
of a purple umbrella
and the availability
of a million damp
leaves.
     This door says

    Storage: mp3 converter, memorial
        day sale, hundreds of extras, life-long value,
        fitness advantage, untapped dollars. Pay

  attention
        to the changes
        in a garden, broccoli
        blue then bluer, shift
        of squash blossom
        filling, ragged
        tomato leaf,
        ribbons

  of long, cool corn leaves   and

      no   end   no
        end   no

            end

FINISH/
UNFINISH

I guess I'm looking for a path. I guess

I'm looking
to be buried

       in the trees secretly I like
       getting lost secretly

so I can find
myself
       again secretly

water the garden all
       the way

       down secretly if you squeeze

the grass, sun
will fill up your fists secretly

       tell me about yourself.

Relinquish

yourself and redeem
the path.

TWO NOVEMBERS

The loveliness of this unending rain,
November, Rebecca's wet, black eyes,
night, the fact of things: wine and
funny - colored berries, sand - colored
crust under the apples. Deanna's hands
around the music and what enters
us all. Rain, a window made of rain and
the rainy skin of rain, the soaked texture
of laughter and our slanted reflection
letting the texture take over.

~

This road leads to November,
                             unfinished
chores, ice floes in my teeth,
                     frozen
trees, the men I'll never know in the
                               garden
he kicks the frozen dirt says the word,
                               "verdant,"
then, "birds." So much darkness, he
                     cried
for half an hour in the dream I
                             kissed him.

ALMOST THANKSGIVING,
UNSTEADY

    Thelma

at the top of the street, is sweeping. The wind feels good
a little bit around her neck, the hair inside her collar
just starting to sweat. She likes it out here. Nobody
tells her what to do, not too many questions, not too much
to talk about.

    Thelma
    is sweeping.

*They be here.... sister...brother...cousin. they be here...
pretty soon... take me... far away... take me... overnight
they be here.*
    Swoosh. Swoosh.

The wind shifts and suddenly leaves explode
in all directions. Thelma leans closer to the broom,
brushes a small pile efficiently from the curb. Wipes
her mouth on her sleeve. She's got that dirty parka on.

    Thelma
    is waiting.

*What if they mean?...men at the institution, mean...mean
with mean faces...walk around mean with lotta keys...
what if they mean?*

    Thelma
    sweeps   and sweeps.

                    Thelma
is a buried shape inside the wind.   Thelma
is a scared mole-shape stuck in the cold, grey sky.
She slides past my window, her deep greasy eyes
looking in. She wants the comfort of whatever's
inside. She's afraid, too. She's drawn to the heat,
the drama. She wants no part of it. She can do it
alone.

             Thelma is sweeping.

             Swoosh. Swoosh.

             Thelma

takes a broom from every neighbor on Buell Street.
She tries one from each stoop, side door, or tool shed.
But she always brings them back – even the ones with
just a handful of bristles or splintered handles. She
brings them back and puts them carefully away. She
knows how to do it. She's a strong woman. She is
"in control." Thelma Chapford controls this
neighborhood. She is the honcho with a broom.

             Swoosh. Swoosh.

             Thelma
             is sweeping.

The wind sharpens, up from the lake. Thelma shoves
her shoulders deeper into her parka, tightens her hood
under her chin. She has to squint now to see the few
shadows that might be leaves. Mostly, she feels the
muscles in her arms moving and listens as the bristles
scratch the pavement. Back and forth. *Swoosh.
Swoosh.* A couple other lights come on in the street.

Thelma   is sweeping.

*They be here...they're sneaky. Sneaky like soap operas...
they're sneaky and smilin'...they took me that place...
how long ago?..will they bring me back? how long is a day?*

Almost
Thanksgiving, unsteady
Thelma

at the bottom of Buell Street, still sweeping. From
the window, Thelma is more blur now than shape, more
moving than longing. She stops for a minute and looks
up toward the window. But she's got that broom.

Swoosh.

I HAVE THE SUNSET, PINK

through the wire of my iPod, a shudder
        of fire and blood behind
silk. Three green lights
        in a row prove accidents
do happen. In one's hand
        are enough genetics
to get a little heat till something
        cools beneath the street,
and birds collide with
        footfall which reminds me to
resume that talk with my ancestors.
        Upward, the tall pines notice,
I am this fragrance, too.

WITH EVERYONE

I go there
> because I have a three-
> year-old
> at home, a desk full
> of uncharted
> data, something desperately
> I have to work out.

The white toe
> of a Nike running shoe
> appears in the bottom of a chlorine
> blue, wall-sized mirror. Soon a sea
>
> of toes is awake
> in the glass, up
> and down with ping-
> pong regularity: thigh work.

There is order
> here, yet also a strange
> permissiveness. Light from the mirror
>
> catches wet spots
> on the lavender sweat pants
> beside me. Sweat
> here held
> in high esteem. Was it
>
> the thought of a gym bag
> that first drew me here? Its robust
>
> contents testimony
> of process? (I ain't
>
> done yet) or the democracy
> of a locker room? Mostly

    it's subliminal.
        I go there to reckon:
            my weakness,
            my strengths.

    I go there to appear
        and disappear
        with everyone.

Touch the shadow in the closet, blurt

"BUT WHAT DO YOU CALL IT?!" All

that snow sealing you in the dream. Jesus,
the reason they don't live in it is it's a
funeral home! The recessed rooms, cups,
bowls and saucers are all spray-painted to match
the deceased's coloring. And the back part's
nothing but a drafty factory for the long gone.
It's a vista of snow and ice; it stings
someone's stained face. It's a mirror, the past
patched there like broken glass. Can't see
beyond that, just the shadows formally
opening. I finally understand.

Here, the view opens and is my own strength.

Winter

AT THE STUDIO

She decided that when she got there
she would be okay. Like a place
could do that: Like
a place could arrange
her for her. She
came for the time.
She came for the backdrop, the back-track,
the end run, the redress,
the sideways.
She came to watch. She came for the time
to watch.

~

    I'm down here
    where nothing is lonely. I'm down
    here where
    all is forgiven. I'm down here
    where everything is given
    a theme-
    song and a rhythm,
    a lean letter-
    opener, a narrow
    blade of licorice
    a choice.

AH, TO THINK OF RILKE IN THE LOCKER ROOM

while my hair grows, January
at bay, limbs
coaxed
and glistening with heat
and moisturizer,
the world miles away, lovely
miles away. Here
the blow-dryer lifts every hair lovingly
and with enlarged
solitude.

Rilke, I think you'd understand. Sometimes

I sit in the sauna and pretend
that my life is over. It's not
unpleasant — all those events, just
so much *fa-dee-la*. What
was the fuss?

Then
it surfaces, Rilke, just like you said,
what was sunken is indeed
ample and dusky, and naked
with other women on the warm, cedar planks,
we sweat, we don't
discuss anatomy, but speak tenderly,
watchful and glad
in each other's

difficult search. Rilke,
I think you would approve -- the silence
among us

and the silence becoming
the lovely life
miles away.

Rainer Maria Rilke (1875-1926) was an Austrian poet whose famous letters recommend the cultivation of a rich inner life.

REACH
ECSTASY

        how?

                close the door
                take your time.

first thing in morning:

    toilet paper
    brushes against
    African violets.

    YOU   WILL   FIND   YOURSELF

  immersed   in a tub   of   tepid   grey   water.

            it will probably be winter

and your day off,

        maybe music   alone
            with the pretty ladies'
            voices.

the gentle throb
of neighbors
talk through the wall.

        INHALE: (chest) over water
        EXHALE: (chest) under water
EMERGE.

    say what you want to.

WHY I LOVE YOUR FACE, *for Lizzie*

Because it is sleepless.

> The creases
> from the fragile, moon-
> covered linens
> have printed it with special
>
> underwater intelligence
> and it's radiant.

It is not.
> Because it's transparent.

> Because of the intricate
> > castle of smoke
> > that surrounds it.

> Because you built it.

Because it is measured   managed
> and   pulled.

> Because it is not.

> Because it's a nest
for your laughter and the ongoing

> shadows of history.

> Because of how open.

> > Because it is weary.

> Because of the light.

> > Because it doesn't lie.
> Because it hasn't been easy.

YELLOWED SUN

    behind
    window shade.

Which is older? Sun or shade?

    Answer slow.
        Yellowed sun
      or window
shade? Daylight knocks
on the roof.

DRAWING CLASS MODEL

I am fixed
at the center of you, group
of watching heads.

You unease me.
Your eyes scratch my surface.
You question me:
Mute
animal eyes.
How can I answer?

My lips are a squiggle
for you to trace.
How can I speak?

I am frozen.
I am Isis, some
kind of statue, immobile
I embody
something
that makes your hands twitch.

You fidget
for me, back and forth, jerk,
nerves more and more, sight
inside you a peculiar
adrenalin. You can't

stop now. You

approach the passive
white page like a lover, bashful
yet earnest, hands
tentative
at first, feeling
it out, gentle
searching for the whole

song behind silence, then
stronger   yes

I can feel it.
Go on
       (don't forget
more, more
            my heart.

THE VISIT/ OLD FRIEND, LOST

Her hands on the steering wheel: I can see her hands on the steering wheel. Somewhere in this tangled Florida interstate, her hands. It is right that she live here among so many blossoms. The sea is another blossom, sprawled and continual, the slow lull of a whisper. With hibiscus and disarrayed palms, her hands. Alone in my car, I clutch my map. The place we're to meet crawls there in blue and red. From a bridge, weird primordial birds plunge, sun-scalded, into the glossy waves — a sudden shape, all want. It takes a lot of tongue to say the word "lush." Lemon tree, magnolia, thick lizards on the salty earth. Her hands. Her hands endeared her to me — her long white hands feeling for something always made of air.

VACANT SKY

When I was a child questioning the great vacant
sky,
the father of silence and forever I
could also hear the long
awful call
of the diesel trucks
churning in the distance. Disturbed, I
thought
the trucks were
gods
and angry at
men or me, and even
now there is a sound
that keeps my head tilted, shoulders
asking is there
something
just farther than I can see,
large as an explosion or the sprawling

  shape of weather?   It smells
like instinct.
        It insists
        I believe.

THE EVOLUTION

of my father's soul
is trudging up the hill,

comforting
like the sound
of the lumbering

recycling truck, coming
around again. Lumbering,
persistent and unfinished.

Thank God
slow learners get a second chance

and all opposites
long to trade places. I can't
remember

if language poets use words
or not. Or if
they confess.

I do. I don't
normally put my hands
that far into it.

Surrender.
                    Surround.

BREATH/
WORK/
BIRDS

Here
    it is always winter.
The neighborhood chimneys are little brown birds

      who puff up some song,
                    some
                        song.
The notes they bring up
        turn to smoke
        &
        bales
        &
        bales of

        wet, dark hay.

WASHING WHITE

mugs in winter.
    Dishwater
        grey/
        sky/grey

    wan winter light
wet sundown,
    flooded sky.

Labille Guiard — mixed media

THE MUSIC OF THEIR NAMES
Litany To Be Read Aloud

Sofonisba.   *Sofonisba Anguissola*   *Sofonisba.*
Gentileshi.   *Artemisia Gentileshi.*   *Gentileshi.*
Lavinia.   *Lavina Fontana.*   *Fede Galizia.*
Judith Leyster   *Elisabeta Sirani.*   *Sofonisba.*

    If you haven't heard theses names before it's
    no wonder.

    Think of them as music.
    Think of them as sound. No,

    think of them as little
    pieces of the past retrieved

    over a long afternoon. Think
    of the gathering.

    Think of them as friends.
    Think of them as enemies.

    Think of them as real people,
    their lives lived like

    anyone's – one regular
    day at a time.

Sofonisba.   *Gentileshi.*   *Lavinia.*   *Galizia.*

    Think of what was forgotten.
    Think of how to find it again.

    Think of what was given
    up, think of what was left
    out.

Lavinia.   *Sofonisba.*   *Gentileshi.*   *Artemisia Gentileshi.*

*These are names of prominent women artists from 14-16th century European Renaissance. As recently as 1986, HW Janson's *History of Art,* the standard text used in college art history courses, did not include one woman artist.

NO MORE PRAGMATIC NOTES

Do this, fix that, not that,
except please find the large

>   green book jam-
>   packed
>   with secret open

places, gradual
stretches, sketches,

fragments, trillings. Look up

miscellaneous momentary
flashes
divide
and investigate.

>   Or should I say sing?
>   Not
demand. Name, not duty.

Blend, not enumerate. Nuance, not neaten.
The green book is not a task.
My job is unfold.

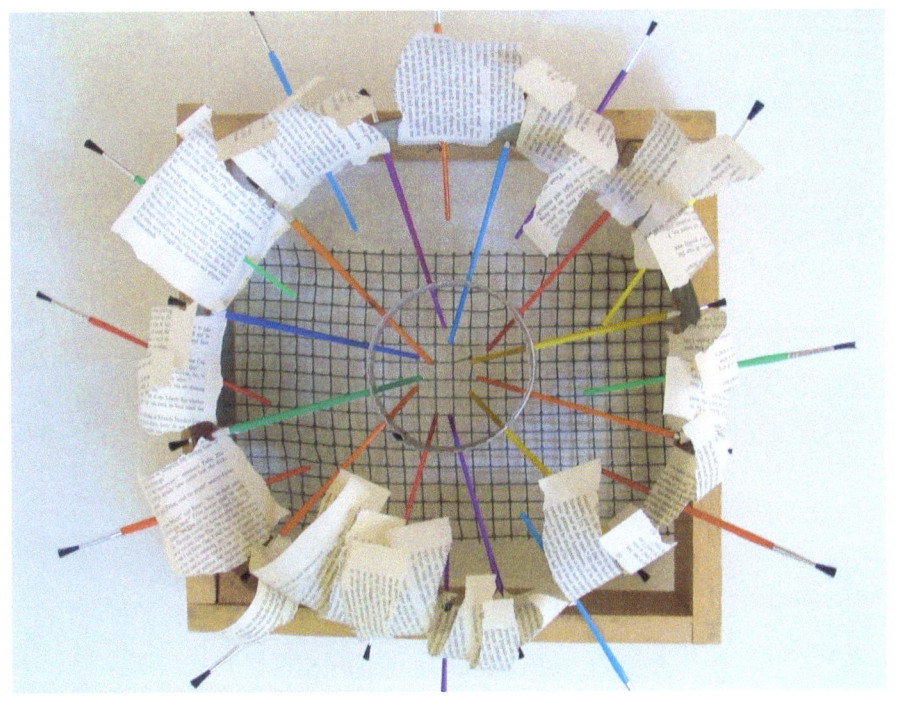

Paintbrush Wheel — mixed media

RESISTANCE

You are still
here. It is nightfall. From
the window you can see
the leaves are no longer
leaves but black sponges, damp
against the draining
sky.

You are safe here.
The pines are a
sturdy fortress
against the strong
north wind. They move
constantly like strange,
brooding echoes.
The house sits firmly
in the overgrowth
of centuries.

It is fine here.
You imagine mice,
worms, squirrels and
hundreds of watching
insects while
the dark comes down
like a lid. The
woods wait – cave
upon cave of
shadow
and silence.

You can be sure here.
There is no reason
to believe that at any
moment it will all
come apart,
burst
into switch-
blades, bright
and ready to cut, but
you do.

THE MOON IS A STILL

frozen target tonight, glossy
as a plate. The moon
is a good, solid
vision, a snow-
ball, hard
and symmetrical,
a fist,
a pearl
buttoned
to darkness.
The moon is a spout-
like opening in the sky.
Madness and the silver
filings of reptiles
pour out.
The moon is a silent
open-faced traveler with
no trousers.
The moon is a bullet
of smooth, runny light,
belligerent
and excessive.
Mostly
the moon is useless
except as defiance
and I can say nothing
about this moon.

NAPKIN POEMS

I would like to eat the entire rack of geraniums.
Live in the flesh. Eat; the color is flesh.

~

A cat walks with no sound.
A cat walks with the same sound as sunlight.

~

Move through the temperatures in the house.
Each unlocks a smell. Each unleashes.
Your body is touch and release.

~

What was that dream? Something about standing
and a mother. Something about a mother and a stem.

~

Stopped in my tracks: Her laugh matched the color
of the sky, her clothes a milky embrace.

~

What I said exactly in the dream was
"Do you want me to cut the stem off that bleeding heart?"

~

Every tree is a waterfall of silence.

~

Fingering plastic six-packs of plants in front of K-mart
in chilly May rain. You want them to fall into your hands
like a sign. You want just the right ones, by accident.

~

Look at that bank of unbelievable snow. Infinite parking lot.
Climb.

~

Weather reports the ceiling unlimited.
This sky is roof for you. Shingles at dawn.

~

Something's shifted in the closet, the mood is different now.
The hooks are hung with thick, somber hues.
Thoughtfully, open a soda.

~

The dark is a cold, silent bell around you.
Finger each star.

~

April makes pretty women carrying birthday cakes.
The white skin on the back of their necks freed in the white,
white air. Necklace of grass.

~

The backyard pines conspire
and lean together, make
a tea of shadow and the light.

~

It's a heart. It's a door. A heart. A door.

~

Listen: the magenta door is the heart of your story.
Sudden opening – surprise boundary –
necessary push. You need
to go through it.